1 IN 4 WOMEN & 1 IN 6 MEN WILL HAVE BEEN SEXUALLY ABUSED BEFORE THE AGE OF 18.

This means that there are more than 42 million adult survivors of child sexual abuse in the US.

The primary reason that the public is not sufficiently aware of child sexual abuse as a problem is that 73% of child victims do not tell anyone about the abuse for at least a year, 45% of victims do not tell anyone for at least 5 years, and some tell much later in life because it is too painful for the conscious mind to deal with, so it is repressed.

In addition, sometimes they go to their deaths with this secret and sometimes the secret is the cause of death. Evidenced in the fact that a meta-analysis of 9 studies from 6 different countries, with a total of almost 9000 participants, showed that those who experienced childhood sexual abuse before the age of 16 to 18 years were more than twice as likely to attempt or complete suicides. (Indicated by data from several sources.)

OTHER BOOKS BY THE AUTHORS

James F. Miller

NEON LIGHTS

LIFE, DEATH AND MAN BETWEEN

Jerry Miller

EMPTY SPACE:
Creating A Theatre In
Your Church Step-By-Step
(Amazon.com)

To my sister Sallie,
For having protected me
from my self
                 - Jim

Dedicated to my loving grandfather,
M.M. Churchwell,
after whom I was named
                 - Jerry

Abused. Addicted. ALIVE!

THE DAY THE RAIN CAME DOWN

THE STORIES OF GAY IDENTICAL TWINS

BY JIM & JERRY

James F. Miller & Jerry M. Miller

Jerry M. Miller, Publisher
Chicago, IL
email: gaev5@yahoo.com

Ordering Information:
Quantity sales. Special discounts are available on quantity purchases by corporations, associations, and others. Orders by U.S. trade bookstores and wholesalers. Please contact Jerry Miller by email at: gaev5@yahoo.com

Printed in the United States of America

Publisher's Cataloging-in-Publication data
Miller, James F. & Miller, Jerry M.
The Day The Rain Came Down: The stories of gay identical twins /
James F. Miller, Jerry M. Miller.
p. cm. 160 pages. 6 x 9 inches. 15.24 x 22.86 centimeters
Library of Congress Control Number: 2017917421
ISBN-13: 978-1-979451-22-2
ISBN-10: 1-979451-22-2
1. Self-Help. 2. Recovery. 3. 12 Steps

First Edition

Editing, cover design, book design: Valentino Zubiri
Contact valzubiri@gmail.com for your book projects

Display fonts used:
Multicolore by www.neogrey.com, ivan@neogrey.com
Stroke by The Kinetic, Estian Fourie, www.thekinetic.co.za info@thekinetic.co.za

Abused. Addicted. ALIVE!

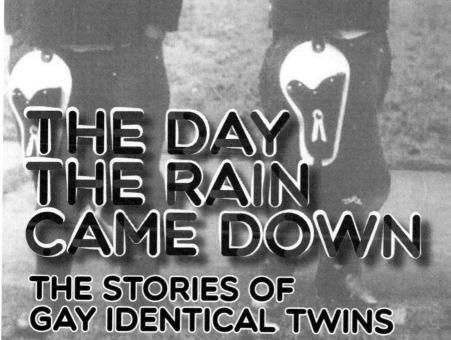

THE DAY THE RAIN CAME DOWN

THE STORIES OF GAY IDENTICAL TWINS

BY JIM & JERRY

James F. Miller & Jerry M. Miller

TABLE OF CONTENTS

PREFACE

Everyone has a story. These are our stories.

We want to tell our stories later in life, because now there are fewer chapters to be lived.

If the chapters were written too early, we might not convey the joy of growing and learning and moving beyond the dark chapters. Our favorite quote is "It is always darkest before the dawn."

We sometimes wish that our stories did not include sexual abuse, bullying as young gay men, alcoholism, compulsive gambling, compulsive spending, sex addiction and nicotine addiction. There are parts of our stories that are dark and brutally frank. We don't mean to offend but want to tell the truth. To talk about the secrets that we were not supposed to tell.

We hope that our stories and our experience, strength and hope will serve as an inspiration to others. We know in our heart of hearts that there is always hope and light. The demons and principalities and powers will not win out.

We are eternally grateful for the countless people who have shared their experience strength and hope with us. Their stories have kept us alive.

- Jim and Jerry

INTRODUCTION

Patrick J. Carnes, Ph. D., the noted author and psychologist on sex addiction recovery, says in his book, *A Gentle Path through the 12 Steps:*

> *"Addicts and co-addicts typically have a problem feeling safe. Many were sexually, physically or emotionally abused; others lived for years in an environment of fear, trauma, or continual stress. Such an environment causes the brain to produce powerful neuro-chemicals known as cortisol and endorphins... These chemicals then become two of the main drivers of addiction.*[1]

> *"Each of us has an internal narrative about our life. We use this narrative as a way to see the world and explain it to ourselves. For addicts, this story typically involves fear, shame, victimization, blame and anger. The more we retell this story to ourselves, and the more we see the world through the filter of our narrative, the deeper we dig the painful and ha-*

---

1. Patrick J. Carnes, Ph.D., *A Gentle Path through the Twelve Steps Updated and Expanded, The Classic Guide for All People in the Process of Recovery* (Center City, MN: Hazelden Publishing, 2012), 9.

bitual neural pathways in our brain. This keeps us locked in our addiction and in our repetitive, dangerous patterns of behavior.

"Recent science has revealed that we can literally change our brain by retelling our story so that it includes new perceptions, new understandings and new conclusions. As we rewrite our story, we rewire our brain by building new, more functional neural pathways. Over time, as we continue to retell this new story to ourselves and others, we strengthen and deepen those pathways providing ever more support for our healing and recovery."[2]

Telling our story also encourages the elemental human experience of bonding. In bonding, we open ourselves to others and build trust, attachment, empathy and vulnerability.

---

2. Carnes, *A Gentle Path through the Twelve Steps*, 10.

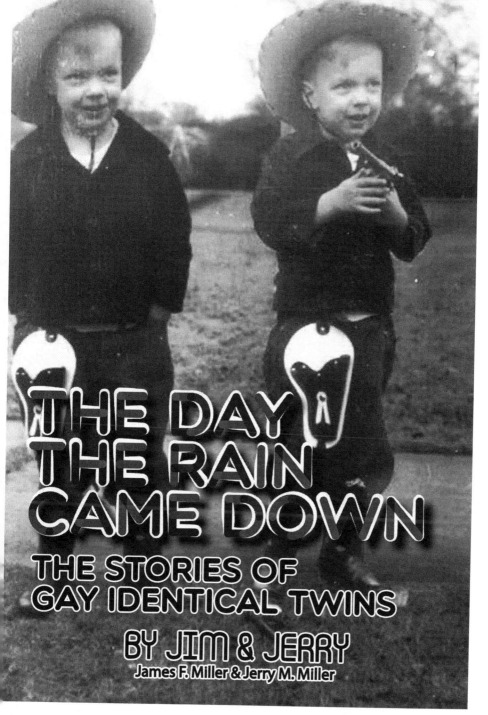

Abused. Addicted. ALIVE!

THE DAY THE RAIN CAME DOWN

THE STORIES OF GAY IDENTICAL TWINS

BY JIM & JERRY

James F. Miller & Jerry M. Miller

James F. Miller
Yellow Flowers, Red Background, 1980s
acrylic on paper, 12" x 9"

James F. Miller
Coyote Design, 1990
acrylic on paper, 12" x 9"

FAMILY BEGINNINGS

My twin brother Jerry and I were born May 6, 1945 in Schumpert Memorial Sanatorium in Shreveport, Louisiana.

Five months later, my family moved to Oklahoma City, Oklahoma. This included my older sister Sallie, my older brother, my twin brother Jerry, my mother, and my father.

My family lived in a four-bedroom house in a middle class neighborhood. Down the street from our house was a large park with a tall concrete fountain. In the summer our sister took us to the park and we waded in the fountain. In the winter she took us snow sledding.

At Easter time, my twin and I had baby chickens that were dyed different colors and didn't live very long. We also had a rabbit and a dog named Junior who was part cocker spaniel and part dachshund.

We attended an elementary school that had a carnival

every year. They had a cakewalk and I remember winning a chocolate cake in the cakewalk, and a lamp in a drawing.

There were two bedrooms in the back of our house. My older brother occupied one and my parents the other. My twin brother and I shared an old four-poster bed in the middle of the house.

I slept on the window side of the bed in the bedroom that I shared with my twin.

There was an attic fan located in the hallway that blew fresh breezes in the window. I kept the window open and enjoyed smelling the rain during evening showers.

My sister occupied the front bedroom. But when my older brother moved to the separate servant quarters outside the house, my sister moved into my older brother's bedroom. I was moved into this front bedroom of my sister.

THE DAY THE RAIN CAME DOWN

- *Jim*

Papa

Papa sneaking in,

In the middle of the night, And climbing

    into bed, And not letting go,

And I wanting to know where mama was.

    Waking up in empty rooms,

And empty beds, With nameless men, Sore

    and bruised, And feeling used,

And never knowing love.

Steamy rooms and swimming pools, And

    sunken baths,

Dark encounters, Porno films,

And toilet stalls,

Head and hand strokes, To countless cars.

And never knowing love.

**Homemade birthday cake from our Grandmother
Jesse when Jim and Jerry turned 5 in 1950**

ABUSE

I don't know what night it happened. I believe that I was about 11 years of age. My father came into my bedroom in the middle of the night and climbed into bed with me. He held me in a spoon fashion and would not let me go. After a couple of hours he went back to the bedroom my mother and he shared.

After this, he returned to my bedroom once a week. I wasn't able to sleep at night until the wee hours of the morning for fear of him returning back into my bedroom. I was petrified. I froze whenever he came back and held me tight with his arms. I remember the smell of semen on his blue silk pajamas.

I knew by the age of ten that I was gay. My father told me that gays were less than scum and if anyone found out I was gay that it would destroy the family. At the age of 15 he sent me to a psychiatrist. The psychiatrist told me that gays lead meaningless lives and he personally would never have a gay person in his house.

In junior high school, my peers called me "faggot" and "queer." At the same time, my father, at home, was also sexually abusing me. To escape, I drew imaginary pictures of animals to play with. My father so convinced me that the only way to get loved by a man was to orally service him.

From twenty to thirty years of age, I had serviced over one hundred men.

I did not meet my own sexual needs in these relationships, nor experience any expressions of love from these men nor for myself.

My father made fun of my body. He asked me one day as he was looking at me taking a shower, "Why don't you have a bigger penis?"

It took me years to be able to take a shower once a week. I also wore my clothes to bed out of fear that my father would come in and try to have sex with me.

At 65 years of age, my twin sent me books on childhood abuse. I related to the stories in these books and could no longer deny that my father abused me physically, emotionally and sexually. Someone who was supposed to love me used me.

When I was 66 years old, I confronted my mother about the abuse and why she did nothing. She gave me an article about how psychologists planted in their patients' minds that they had been abused. Mother was in her late 80s.

Later I forgave my mother for not doing anything.

During that period of time, had she left my father, she would not had been able to work and make enough income to take care of four children.

Some professionals say that the more the abuse on a child, the more addictions are developed by that person. Today, since there is more awareness of abuse, perhaps people can face the abuse and receive help at an earlier age.

For me, I developed five addictions: alcoholism, substance abuse, gambling, nicotine and compulsive sex. I am now 72 years old.

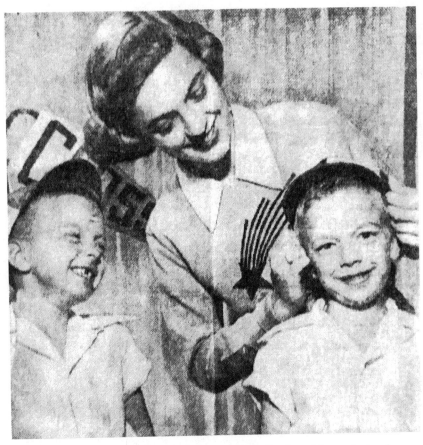

Jim and Jerry as mascots for their older sister's high school pep club

ALCOHOLISM

I remember my mother giving me a sip of beer when I was five years old.

I can still experience the taste of that beer.

In my sophomore year in high school, my friends and I would go to drive-ins drinking "3 point 2" beer smuggled in from Texas. There wasn't enough beer to go around to get drunk. "Three-two beer" or "3 point 2 brew" is low-point beer that contains 3.2% alcohol by weight.

In my senior year, a friend of mine and I bought a pint of vodka and got drunk.

It was the first time that I found something that took away the pain from my father's abuse. I postponed my drinking career to get a major in Journalism and a minor in English.

I was on the Dean's Honor Roll, an Outstanding Independent Student, and treasurer of the senior class. I had no friends and felt empty and hollow. I began to take menial jobs and get drunk. I had no confidence in my talent as a journalist and a writer.

It took me 44 years to admit I was powerless over alcohol. Yet, alcohol also stopped working to make me forget. It no longer took away the pain of what my father did to me. Yet, though I tried to quit, I could not.

I tried changing jobs, friends, and places to live. I even tried taking a vacation. One evening, a friend of mine who worked with me as a waiter in a local restaurant, came by.

He told me that he had been going to 12-Step meetings. He noticed all the beer cans on the floor and let me know that I should call him if I wanted to go to a meeting. I did not call him, but I went to a meeting the next night. I was told, that since it was my first meeting, that I could not go into the main meeting hall. I had to go to a Step One, Two, Three meeting in a smaller room.

In the smaller room, there were people who had suffered a broken nose, leg or arm.

I did not want that to happen to me. The next night, I was welcomed into the big room.

My friend gave me a Big Book and said he would be my sponsor. The Big Book is the "basic text" for a 12-Step group for alcoholics.

He told me to read the section that had the doctor's opinion that explained that alcoholism was a disease. I had always thought I was just a bad person. I had thought I was immoral and could not use my own will to quit. On the second day that I was sober, I woke up crying. I asked "someone," "somewhere," to take this shit away from me. After this, the obsession to drink went away.

I watched 365 movies on my first year of my sobriety. My 12-Step sponsor used to take me to lunch and I listened to what he said, but was unable to respond. I was too much in withdrawal from alcohol.

This changed later. I improved. I became able to relate to people and communicate.

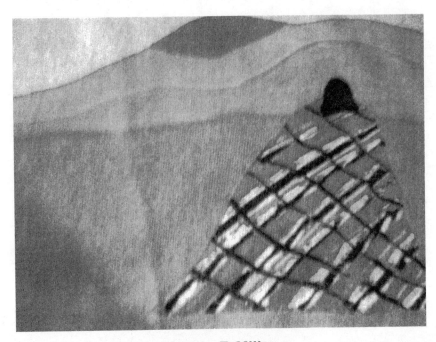

James F. Miller
Santa Fe Woman, 1980s
silkscreen on fabric, 9" x 12"

DRUGS

The first drugs that I tried were Quaaludes. I found out later that they were muscle relaxants. All they did was make my legs rubbery. They didn't get me high.

Then a couple that I knew turned me on to Valium.

The wife was a stewardess. She smuggled in high dosages of Valium from other countries. I tried them and it was like being in love with the whole world.

On another occasion, another friend and I went to a club. I took two Valiums and ordered a Black Russian. A girl came over and asked me to dance. I was shy and gay, yet I danced an erotic dance with her called the "alligator."

My next experimentation with drugs was in college. My neighbors across the hall smoked joints that were the size of cigars. What they said when they were high made no sense at all. I smoked a couple of joints. Smoking pot gave me the munchies for food. When I sat down to work on my stories, the words made no sense.

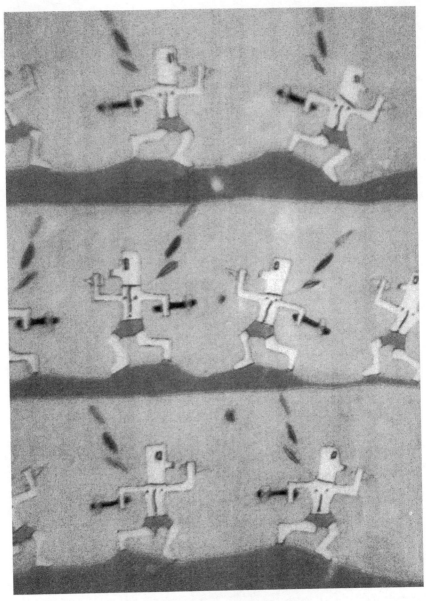

James F. Miller
Running Kachinas, 1980s
acrylic on paper, 12" x 9"

My best friend of that time, Ray, and I went to 12-Step meetings together. We also did a lot of other things together. We had lunch together and went to the movies. My friend liked to bowl and I bought him a fancy agate bowling ball. We also played racquetball and he won most of the time.

One day Ray showed up at my door drunk. I was devastated. I hadn't seen him at meetings recently, and when I called and left messages, he did not return my phone calls. He asked me to bring another gay person over, and he told both of us that he thought he was gay. He also shared that he had been molested by an uncle when he was around twelve.

It didn't matter to me whether Ray was gay or straight. What mattered to me was that he was getting drunk everyday. I thought Ray was just pretending to be gay so he would have a place to stay. He didn't have a car and asked if he could stay with me. I said, "Yes," because I loved him.

Ray was drinking a fifth of bourbon a day and I had no interest in alcohol. Since Ray was not working, he would go to his parents' house and do some work for his father so he could bring home some groceries. Ray was a great cook.

I was attending college at the time, working on a Masters in Education. After class one evening, I had a slip and fell on an unsecured mat outside the college building's front door. I wound up with a bulging disk and a pinched sciatic nerve. It was so bad I wasn't able to get out of bed for 8 months.

My doctor prescribed morphine. Morphine took away the pain so that I was able to function. I was on pain-killers for four months, but they did not help with the pain. Once I lost two morphine tablets so I went without it for two days. Two days later, I had a reaction when I took one. I was on my way to the grocery store and found myself driving badly. A young policeman stopped me and took me to a drug examining station outside the city, in the country. The examining officer said that I was not an addict. The police officer wrote me a ticket for being under the influence.

One night, while Ray and I were watching movies, Ray asked if he could kiss me. I said yes, and he kissed me once, and then again. He said we could make it together, but all he ever wanted was to be serviced, and that was the extent of our sexual relationship.

One other night, Ray secured some ecstasy. I agreed to take one, and that began the end of my clean time. I still didn't desire alcohol. I started mixing morphine, Percocet, Tylenol 3, and hydrocodone. My doctor gave me prescriptions for all four of these drugs. I traded them in exchange for sex or other drugs.

Ray convinced me to let a crack addict stay on the floor for a portion of the rent. I allowed him to stay, but eventually the crack addict was doing drug deals at my kitchen table day and night.

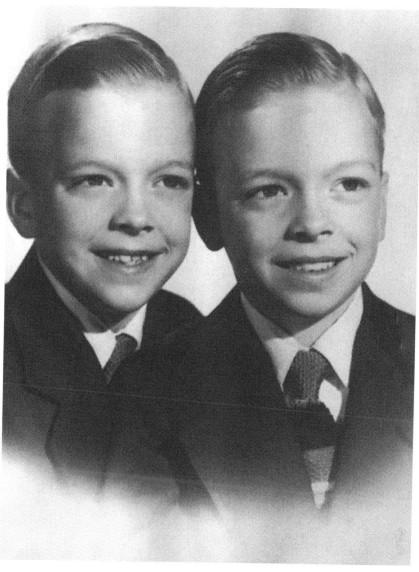

Jim & Jerry, Style Show, 1957

James F. Miller
Santa Fe Cactus, **1980s**
detail of a ceramic tile, 5" x 5"

I once wrote a fake prescription for Tylenol 3 and took it to the pharmacy. The pharmacist said that it looked like a different signature than my doctor's, and he turned me to the police. The jail time for writing a fake prescription was eight to twelve months, but since this was my first drug offense, I was sent to drug court. I had to see my parole officer every week as well as give urine samples once a week. I was able to graduate from drug court.

After I graduated from drug court, I started using drugs again. I stole two hundred dollars worth of groceries from the supermarket in order to eat.

While I was high on drugs one night, I drove my Mustang Convertible into a utility pole. By this time, I had two or three crack addicts sleeping on my living room floor.

One day, my sister showed up and told me that we were going to the hospital. I told the doctor that I wasn't doing any drugs. He said the substances in my body proved me wrong.

My former therapist and my sister were able to admit me to a treatment center. It was a three-month program at the Colorado State Mental Hospital.

I attended classes at the hospital forty hours a week. There were people in the program who didn't graduate and are now facing twenty to thirty years in prison. It was one of the toughest treatment centers in the United States, but they also had recreational activities. There was an Olympic-style swimming pool, a bowling alley, and a pool table. We also had field trips to baseball games, were hosted to ice cream socials, and were taken to watch the fireworks on the Fourth of July. I graduated with honors. That was the real and final end of my drug career.

GAMBLING

When my father died at age 68, my mother sold his office supply company. To celebrate the sale, she took my brother and I on a weekend trip to Las Vegas. We stayed at the Stardust Hotel on the Strip. My mother spent her time playing blackjack. My twin decided to play the slots. My twin and I were in our 30s.

I took my chances on roulette. For four days I fluctuated between losing and winning. On the last day of our trip, I was down to my last ten dollars. I bet the ten, and soon turned that into one thousand dollars. I gave my mother the thousand dollars and told her to hang on to it for me.

Our next trip to Las Vegas was for the opening of the Mirage Hotel and Casino. It was a fancy place. Behind the desk where we registered, there was a 20,000-gallon aquarium with baby sharks.

On our first night there, we went to see the incredible Siegfried and Roy with their beautiful white tigers. Their show that evening was awesome.

The next morning, we had breakfast at the hotel restaurant, and then we were off to gamble again. My mother played blackjack. My twin and I played the slot machines. Every time we had a big win, instead of putting the money aside, we bet to win even bigger. I finally hit one big jackpot and gave the money to my mother. My twin kept losing.

Unlike me he had a credit card and took out over $1,000 which he promptly lost. He went home broke and in debt.

My mother complimented me on saving the money that I won instead of putting it back into the slot machines.

I traveled to Las Vegas two times after that on my own.

I came home broke each time.

When I was working as a waiter in Oklahoma City, I visited the casinos in Kansas City on several occasions.

When I was winning, I called the restaurant where I worked as a waiter and ask someone to cover my shift.

I always put all my winnings back in the slot machines so I always came home broke.

Jim & Jerry, 8th grade, 1961

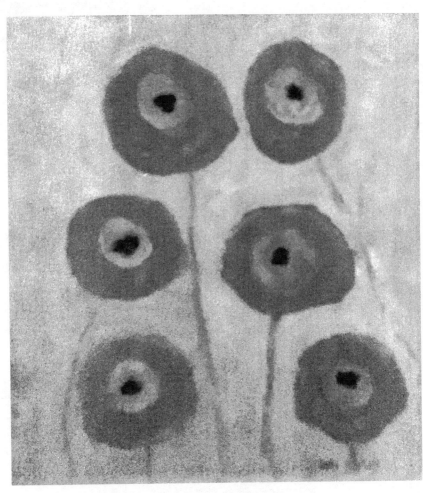

James F. Miller
Blue Flower, 2000s
acrylic on paper, 12" x 9"

DARIAN

I first met Darian at a 12-Step meeting for alcoholism and other 12-Step meetings for additional addictions. We would greet each other and eventually exchanged telephone numbers.

Darian was staying in a halfway house. He told me that his roommate had hung himself and that he needed to get out of there. So I invited him to stay with me and he agreed. He showed me that his track marks from shooting up were beginning to heal.

I was able to get him a job as a busboy at the same restaurant in which I was working. We would attend 12-Step meetings for drugs and alcohol together. One day, his old friends came by my apartment and he went out with them.

I didn't hear from him after that for quite a time. He dropped by one day to show me the needle marks on his hands and feet. He told me that his old friend had talked

Jim & Jerry, seniors in high school, 1963

him into doing drugs and having sex with his wife. He was not living in a crack house.

One of the guys in the crack house asked Darian to shoot him up and Darian could not find a vein to shoot into.

I knew that if Darian stayed at the crack house much longer, he would die. I had to get him out of that place and out of town.

I went and leased a Mustang convertible and we went to Kansas City to get away. We stopped by the crack house on the way out of town so Darian could get his birth certificate so he could show proof of age for drinking and gambling.

When we arrived at the Casino parking lot, Darian started crying and told me that he had lost his best friend. I asked him who that person was, and the told me that it was not a person, but drugs.

We entered the Casino and began gambling. We won $18,000 in three hours.

We spent the summers going back and forth between Kansas City and Oklahoma City.

On another occasion, we won $10,000. We hit three bow ties on a slot machine and won the jackpot.

The employee who cashed us out said that he had never seen anyone hit the jackpot. We also won money from hitting jackpots on the five-dollar slot machines.

By the end of that summer, all the money was gone and Darian went back to drugs. He quit after a week and then returned to 12-Step meetings. Today he is married and has a wife and two kids with red hair, just like his.

Just after all this, I received a call from my sister that my mother was very sick. The doctor told her that she only had a couple of months to live. My sister was working as a Special Education teacher at a high school in Colorado Springs, Colorado. She had used up all her vacation time and sick pay time to take care of my mom. She asked me if I would come home and help her take care of my mother. The people in the restaurant where I worked in Oklahoma City did not want me to move because we were like family, but I decided to move to Colorado Springs to help take care of my mother. I moved in with my mother. Every morning I would greet her with a big "Good Morning!." Her reply was, "What's good about it?"

She was very negative most of the time. I had to force myself to be positive and try to encourage her to be positive. I would take her to the doctor four or five times a week. Each time I took her to a doctor, the doctor would tell me that she was getting better, and she was. She lived another 12 years and died peacefully in her sleep at the age of 97.

It was difficult taking care of my mother. She would lay guilt and shame whenever I left her to go to 12-Step

Jim and Jerry. Cowboy outfits given to us by our Grandad M.M., 1953.

meetings or go out to eat with my friends. She said that she was paying me good money to take care of her and I shouldn't leave her.

I started going to the casinos again. I would travel to a casino about an hour and a half way from Colorado Springs. I would take the money that my mother gave me and my disability check that I received for being bipolar. I would win and then lose and then chase the money that I lost. I was unable to stop gambling. When I finally went to a 12 step group for compulsive gamblers, I learned that my gambling was not about money, but getting an adrenaline rush that started the minute I put a coin in the slot machine.

Whenever I ran out of money, I would embezzle money out of my mother's investment account. I used her credit card and wrote checks to the casino on her account as well. I started with small checks to cover my losses, but this escalated to my writing checks for $5,000.

I would then write a check to my bank to cover my losses. My sister eventually caught me.

My sister also found out about the forged checks and credit card use. She threatened to send me to prison.

My twin brother was already going to a 12-Step group for compulsive gambling. He suggested that I start attending meetings.

He recommended that I move out of my mother's

residence and find my own place.

I attended meetings for ten years, but I decided to celebrate my graduation from drug court by going and gambling at a mountain casino.

I lost my entire disability check and started approaching people begging them for a few bucks. I told them that I was having an unlucky streak.

The police kicked me out of the casino three times. The police finally suggested that I stay away from the casinos for a couple of weeks.

Later, I stole money from the tip jars in front of the casino cages. I was not caught.

One time, I was so preoccupied with gambling that I missed the 2 a.m. bus to Colorado Springs. It was mid-winter and I stood outside one of the casinos waiting for the next bus that wouldn't arrive until 8 a.m.

I picked up cigarette butts on the ground and smoked them. I snuck inside the casino to grab a cup of coffee and eat some free popcorn. The 8 a.m. bus finally arrived.

When I arrived home, I immediately went to bed. In my sleep, all I could hear were the sounds of slot machines.

You would think that I had surely hit bottom by now.

But I had not.

I had money stored up to pay my rent. I also had

enough for the next month's rent. I went back to the mountain casino. In no time, I had gambled away all my money.

I found a player's card that was left on a counter top of the cashier's booth. The card had $250 in points on it.

The lady in the booth told me that it must be lucky day and gave me $250 cash. I immediately lost the $250 in the slot machines.

While I was at the counter getting money from the card, the casino camera took a picture of me. The owner of the card reported that the card was lost. My picture was looked up and I was frisked by security.

Shortly after that, I was arrested for identity theft, which is a felony. The charge was later changed to a misdemeanor, when I was in court before the judge.

I was sentenced to one month in county jail. It was not a bad situation. The jail was nice. People had their own individual cells. The meals were good.

There was a television that stayed on all night. Those jailed could play spades and hearts with other inmates in the common area.

It took me three months to get a court date even though I was sentenced to just one month.

After my release, I started going to the 12-Step group for my gambling. I recently celebrated five years of sobriety from gambling.

COMPULSIVE SEX

My compulsive masturbation began at the age of 11. I would lock myself in the bathroom and masturbate to homoerotic images painted by James Baldwin and Williams Burroughs graphic gay novels.

I practiced this ritual once a week, initially, but it escalated to two or three times a week. By the time I graduated from high school, I was masturbating every day.

In my later years, just like everyone else, I discovered internet pornography. There were pictures of men masturbating or having sex with other males.

There were also chat rooms where you could talk to other men and exchange sexually explicit pictures. Sometimes, I engaged in phone sex with one of these men. After climaxing, I would immediately hang up. This behavior was not very fulfilling.

There were also hookup web sites where you could physically meet with someone and have sex. Often, when

I met these hookups, they were drunk or on drugs. Many were not sure of their sexual identity. Hookup sites were not the place to look for an ongoing relationship.

The Gay Sexual Revolution came in the '60's. Gay bars and gay bathhouses were flourishing. At the baths, you could rent a room for the night and have sex with multiple partners.

This was also the time when HIV was discovered. The baths were closed down. Gay bars came to a standstill.

People became very cautious about having sex with others. They would show their current HIV test results so they could prove that they had been recently tested and that their results were negative for the disease.

While I was in graduate school, my roommates and I held a party for our friends.

My best friend at the party told me that there was a girl named Mary Jo that had gone to my bedroom. When I arrived at my room, Mary Jo was lying naked in my bed. I sat on the edge of my bed and she informed me that we could not have sex then because she was having her period, but she would like to later in the month.

I bought matching sweatshirts with my name on one and hers on the other.

When we finally did have sex, I had an orgasm in about 3 minutes. I was very embarrassed, but Mary Jo told me that it would take time to get used to having sex.

For the next three years, Mary Jo and I drank beer, ate chicken and had sex.

Mary Jo's father was a trust officer at a very large bank. Her parents took weekly trips to other cities. Mary Jo and I would stay at her parents house while they were gone. We cooked meals, got drunk, and had sex in their bed, the shower, and the backyard.

Whenever we went to parties at friends, we would lock the door to the bedroom and have sex. Mary Jo told our friends that she was going to get married soon, but did not tell them that she was marrying me. She later informed me that she had not been taking any birth control pills because she wanted to have a baby with me.

I got scared and told here that I would not introduce her to my parents and we were not getting married. I told her our relationship was over.

I am grateful for Mary Jo allowing me to be sexual with her. I enjoyed every minute of it. But we had nothing in common other than drinking, sex, and liking chicken.

I finally told her that I was gay. She told me that had she known about it earlier, she could have helped me.

Jim and Jerry on their 3rd birthday party, 1948

BIPOLAR DISORDER

I had just finished a year of therapy with a female therapist who had been sexually abused as a little girl by a friend of the family.

We both helped each other heal from childhood abuse. Eventually, she moved out of state and I secured a new female therapist.

After three or four sessions, this next therapist asked me if I ever considered that I might be bipolar. I knew a few things about bipolar disorder but didn't know for sure if I was bipolar or not.

The therapist, after a few more sessions, took me off the antidepressant Lexapro and prescribed two other medications for treating bipolar disorder: Abilify and Paxil.

She prescribed these to help with the symptoms of my bipolar disorder. My symptoms included having delusions of grandeur and sometimes being recklessly sexually compulsive. I also had periods of extreme energy where

I would go for days without sleep. I had hypomania and could be very creative.

After a few months of taking Paxil and Abilify, I found myself not functioning well. I texted a friend from a 7-11 store that I could not function. When I shared this with my mother and brother they took me to the hospital and I was put in the psych ward. I stayed there for a week of observation. They prescribed the drug Geodon which helped me function much better.

On the depression side of bipolar, I suffered from low self-esteem, no motivation, abnormal sleep patterns and thoughts of suicide.

I attended a bipolar support group. I learned a lot from this group about the medicines that they took and which were successful or not. I was helped by the sharing of others about the methods that they used to cope. I was touched by their stories. I felt compassion for them. One woman was hospitalized every two or three weeks. One girl kept cutting her arms with a razor blade. Another woman kept losing her job.

Except for brief periods of time, I am now doing fine. My doctor has added Lithium to my prescriptions as well as Seroquel for sleep. I haven't once had to return to the psych ward of a hospital.

MOTHER

My mother's sister and their mother died of Scarlet fever when she was very young. Her father, remarried and became a high school principal in Norman, Oklahoma.

My mother's father and step-mother's house was located eight blocks from the University of Oklahoma football stadium.

My dad, mom and twin would travel from Oklahoma City to visit my grandfather and his wife in Norman and we would walk to the stadium to watch the University of Oklahoma Sooners football games.

My Grandfather M.M. was cool. When we were 8, he gave my twin brother and I cowboy outfits complete with holsters, guns, and hats. He also gave us well-padded boxing gloves so we could box without ever harming each other. My uncle, who was a professional photographer, took a picture of us in our cowboy outfits.

When my father died, my mother married her child-

Jim & Jerry, age 10, 1955

hood sweetheart. He was her first love and he asked her to marry him when he was in college, but she didn't want to marry him because he was going off to service.

One day, he called her and told her that his wife had died. My mom shared that my dad had also passed away. He came out for a visit in 1979.

Shortly after his first and subsequent visits, they married in 1981. Jerry, my twin brother, performed the ceremony. After their marriage, my step-dad bought my mom a beautiful home in Santa Fe, New Mexico. The house stood on the top of a hill facing the Sangre de Cristo Mountains.

They had a wonderful relationship. They were like teenagers in love even though they were in their late 60s. My stepdad was a wealthy man and showered my mom lavish gifts such as paintings by well known artists, Indian jewelry, and pottery from upscale shops in the city. My mom had never traveled outside the United States, so he took her on trips to Asian and European cities.

Their time was short-lived. My stepdad developed Alzheimer's and died five years after they were married.

My mother continued to live in Santa Fe and co-owned with my sister and my twin brother an art gallery and antique shop on Canyon Road. After the shop closed, she moved into a retirement home in Colorado Springs where, in 1995, she met her third husband. It was around this time when I lived with her for a few years, during the height of my gambling.

In 1996, my mother and her boyfriend eloped to Hawaii. They continued to live in the retirement center until his death from bone cancer in 2000.

My mom eventually moved into an assisted living complex after having many falls in her retirement home unit. She remained there until her death at the age of 97.

FATHER

My father was born in a small town in Norman. His father owned a country store. My dad's picture was prominent on the packaging of the can of coffee that they sold in the store.

My father attended college, but never finished. My father was a salesman. He sold office supplies all his life. My father taught my twin brother and I how to fish, drive a car, and make model airplanes.

But he was abusive and would beat us with a belt and leave welts on our butts that would take two to three weeks to heal.

What he did best was molest me. He owned my sex life for several years, from 11 to 15 years of age.

James F. Miller
Collage of Coyote Designs
1990

WRITING AND PAINTING

My sister had me sit down in her artist studio at the antique shop and art gallery that she co-owned with my mother and twin brother in Santa Fe.

She put a paintbrush in my hand and told me to draw something. I drew a couple of Kachina Dolls. After that I drew cactuses, mountains and sunsets. I called this my "primitive Southwest art period."

I later painted abstract, whimsical pictures of flowers.

I sold the first of my flower paintings at an art show and then sold others to friends.

My first love has always been writing.

In my sophomore year in high school my teacher told me that I wrote well. She recommended that I enter a state essay contest. I didn't think that I was that creative, but I entered the contest anyway. I won!

In my senior year in high school, I published a book of religious poems called *Life, Death and Man Between,* which was listed in TV Guide and reviewed by a local television show. I also served as the editor of my high school newsletter.

I majored in Journalism in college. I was chosen to be the managing editor of the college newspaper. After graduation I moved to Chicago. In Chicago I became a stringer for US and People Magazine. I was also Entertainment Feature Writer for the Chicago Tribune and the Chicago Sun-Times. I went out to find potential stories, write them up and submit them.

The newspapers bought everything that I wrote. The pay was not enough to make a living, but I loved writing them.

Last year, I published *Neon Lights,* a book of poems. The poems are mainly homoerotic. I wrote them over a period of ten years.

TODAY

Today, I am very happy. I have true friends and a host of 12-Step support groups for my recovery from alcoholism, narcotics, gambling and compulsive sex.

I have not had a drink of alcohol in over twenty-five years. I haven't used drugs for seven years. I recently had a pacemaker put in and my cardiologist told me never to smoke again. I have been sober from nicotine addiction for a year. I have not gambled in 5 years. I haven't acted out sexually in four years. I am now 72 years old.

I live in an assisted living complex because I am not able to manage living by myself. My needs are taken care of. I have my medications, I am fed five days a week, and a nurse is on duty 24 hours a day. Travel is provided two days a week to attend a senior day care center where I can participate in activities, have lunch, and do my writing on the center's computers.

I currently live in Colorado where my sister and her

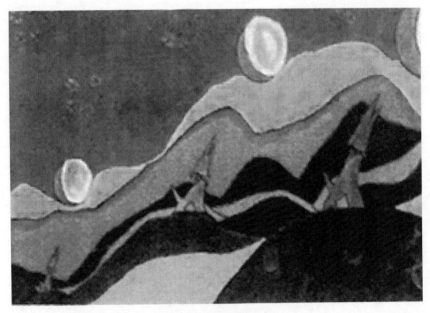

James F. Miller
Coyote Design, 1990
acrylic on paper, 9" x 12"

family live.

I recently went to visit my co-author and twin Jerry over the Thanksgiving Holiday. He lives in a spacious low income senior condo. He pays 30% of his income for rent. I love Chicago and hope to return and live in the city again. I hope to live independently in an apartment like his. Jerry can assist me in finding a place to live independently. Chicago has incredible public transportation and it would be easier to travel to 12-Step meetings, continue my writing, and sell my paintings.

I am currently single but hope to find a partner like my twin has. I am 72 years of age and in good health.

James F. Miller
Coyote Design, 1990
acrylic on paper, 12" x 9"

CLING PEACHES

- Jim

In a sanitorium in Shreveport because there
    were no hospitals there,

I eyed the baby blue and pink beads that
    rested on my thin wrist and spelled my
    name.

I lay on a hand-made quilt full of color, And
    saw the green blades of grass, larger than
    trees around me.

I remember starting to grow deep in the
    South.

Other things, like taste of sulphur, from a
    rusted pipe, along the roadside, captured
    in a pop bottle, and whole green beans,
    snapped in a sink.

Stink bait, mixed in a crock,

Quiet nights with a lantern reflecting over

thin balsa corks with bands of fluorescent
tape, waiting to take the tape,
Broom straws through the brains of catfish
skinned on newsprint on the kitchen
floor,
Doused with lemon and ketchup at Friday
night suppers.
Birthday cakes, on mahogany tables, in
backyards under pecan trees. Wicker
baskets taken off to catch squirrels,
catching only chiggers in smothered out
with fingernail polish.
Attic fans sucking air in and our open
windows in four poster beds, wet rains,
music for slumber,
Black men brawny in humid heat, making
clay-dried bricks in beehive kilns,
Smiling with pearly white teeth.
Rib bowls on the table in Antebellum
homes, buzzers ringing the kitchen from

a foot tapping under the table, and the
maids came.

Crystal clinking, wind blowing sheer muslin
from windows.

Daddy missing the war, drinking, fertilizing
the magnolia tree, and killing it. Boxing
gloves, red wagons, toy lead soldiers and
sandbags burlap tents, scattered across
pine wood floors.

Cling peaches and cream

Watermelons said to have raisins instead of
seeds, homemade ice cream, black eyed
peas, cornbread, okra, upside down cake,
with pineapple if you please.

I grew deep in the South, And now I roam,

Back to home, clinging to peaches, With evil
unknown,

Natural things

In a time long ago.

James F. Miller
Red Flowers, 2000
acrylic on paper, 12" x 9"

ONE-NIGHT STAND

- *Jim*

The phone rings,

I pick it up,

No one talks.

There is no heavy breathing.

In the background I can hear,

Audience laughter

From a TV sitcom show.

I then hear snap

Of a tab on a beer can,

Some gulps

And then a burp.

Then there is a click

And the hum of the phone.

I place my receiver down.

I leave my apartment.

I walk to a corner bar.

I sit on a stool,

Next to an English lady

Who is drinking Russian Vodka.

And speaks Italian.

I order a double bourbon on the rocks.

We visit until the bar closes.

We have nothing in common,

So we go home together.

In the morning I give her

My phone number.

She doesn't call.

Neither does the person who was watching

The sitcom and drinking beer.

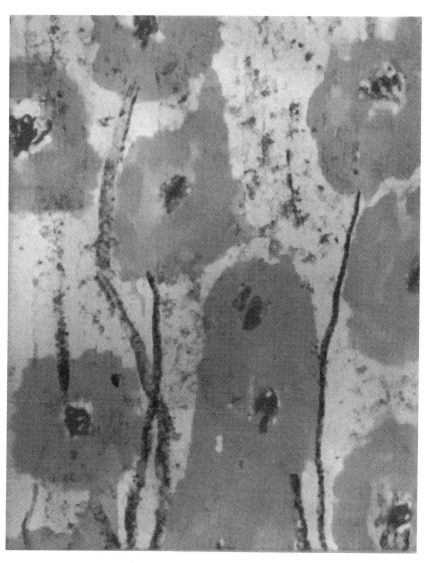

James F. Miller
Yellow Flowers, 1980s
acrylic on paper, 12" x 9"

James F. Miller
Aspens, 1984
acrylic on paper, 18" x 12"

THE STORM

- *Jim*

The Storm is coming.

It begins somewhere inside me.

At first it is just a mere intrusion,

But then the ominous clouds,

Roll over the clear blue sky

Of my happiness,

As if a shadow is appearing

In the corner of my eye,

But then it covers the sun,

Or the moon

If it comes at night

And I cannot see.

It hurts and angers me,

With its injustice and hate

And agues.

I cannot even see you,

And yet you hold my hand,

And wait until it is over,

And after the storm,

The relief of the rainbow comes

And I am alright.

I see clearly now.

You notice the sun,

And the sky in my eyes.

You know I am myself again.

Comfortable in my own skin,

Able to share out of love.

To share with you again.

WINO

- Jim

Sitting in a park bench,

In Central Park.

With a quart of beer

Watching traffic

And passers by

Like a tiger in a cage,

At the zoo

Pacing back and forth

And looking out

Pretending

Like life was about to happen.

EASY LOVE IN A SMALL TOWN

- *Jim*

Easy love in a small town.
Every night Billy Joel would
Come around.

We'd get in his pick-up
Drive to the edge of town,
Park by the big lake,
Hear crickets,
Smell scents of wind-carried
Fresh cut wheat,
Listen to songs,
One station 9.8
Then make love each night
Until very late.

Easy love in a small town,

Not then a girl to be bound.

Now listening to trains overhead,

From the room where I stay,

From the small town,

But still wishing

Billy Joe would come around.

James F. Miller
Bicycles in the Snow, 2009
photograph, 12" x 18"

CRACKER JACKS

- *Jim*

I found you in

My box of Cracker Jacks

Nestled between the full-roasted peanuts

And glossy caramel corn.

Actually I caught your hand,

Groping and pawing

To find my toy

Enraged

I shot you and

Watched you fall over

The kitchen table,

Knocking my box

Of Cracker Jacks,

Peanuts and caramel corn

Were flying everywhere.

Jim & Jerry modeling clothes for the Style Show, 1956

But my toy,

Safely landed on the table,

Relieved,

I picked it up gently

And went into another room,

Dropping a delicate

Paper flower

In a dish of water.

Jerry onstage as a featured performer and producer for a gay cabaret special, Center on Halsted, Chicago, 2010

JERRY

Jerry as Malvolio in Twelfth Night, Santa Fe Shakespeare, New Mexico, July 1991

BEAT UP KID

- *Jerry*

Beat up kid,

No place to run, no place to hide. Boy toy

   used by kin,

Thought he was a sin.

Visitors at night. Couldn't sleep. Boys at

   school,

Wanted help with their manly tool.

Ate in cafeteria alone, Others began to roam,

   To another table,

Unable to eat with a label.

Epitaphs yelled,

On walks to school,

Two black eyes by kid in fear.

Cried. Cause told God don't love queers.

Sex without end, Looking for a friend.

Seeking someone like me, Even paid a fee.

Felt it was time to create the end, Saved by a

    religious friend,

Told me it was the beginning and not the

    end. The best is yet to come,

God says be happy, joyous and free. Hanging

    on a tree,

Spirit will be free.

Father of all will be there for me.

The universe colludes to make dreams come

    true, Hang in there for the journey.

The land of milk and honey.

Calling for me, child of thee, always.

THE EARLY YEARS OF ABUSE

When I was a toddler, my mother told me that I would sit at the breakfast table in our home in a Midwestern city and raise my arms and yell out,

"I love this big, bright wonderful world!"

I did.

I was a curious, outgoing and giving child. I wanted to see what I could bring to others. I was always giving presents to my family, my neighbors and my friends. I liked to bring joy. I wanted everyone to feel loved.

In Vacation Bible School, I learned that Jesus loved all the little children of the world.

There was a poster with a globe and children, representing all the children of the world, positioned around it. I had not met those children of the world. I attended an all-white school and an all-white church except for the black custodian that took care of the church.

There was also a black maid that lived in the servant quarters behind the house of the cattle rancher and his wife who lived across the street from us. The maid's name was Hattie. Hattie would invite me over to the servant's quarters. She let me read her comic books and watch television, and she cooked for me on her single hot plate. We became friends.

While our family was out of town, someone robbed our house of the sterling silver tableware.

The first person accused by my family was Hattie. Racism was very much alive in the small Midwestern town where I lived.

The happy child in love with the world changed after my identical twin, father, mother and older brother abused me sexually, physically, and emotionally.

My twin wanted to show me how to masturbate at around age 11. He attempted to masturbate me with his hand. I told him I didn't want him to do that, but he insisted. This event started an incestuous relationship that lasted until the age of 18.

I was repulsed by the thought that my twin would initiate sex with me, but I liked the pleasure. I was very conflicted and filled with shame and guilt. My twin introduced me to other boys who wanted to have sex with me. I didn't really enjoy it fully, but I liked the pleasure to a degree. I was saddened that my twin was engaging in sex with other boys. I felt abandoned.

My dad also started sexually abusing me at age 11. He asked my older brother, who was 17 at the time, to help him hold me down. He asked my brother to pull my pants and underwear down so he could show him my testicles. My dad said all the men in the family had three testicles. He fondled me trying to show my older brother the three testicles. There was no third testicle.

While my brother and dad were doing this, I was screaming and yelling and trying to get away. My mother yelled from the kitchen and asked what all the yelling was about. My dad told her, "Jerry is just being silly." It was a very violent act against me. I felt trapped, very scared and very sad.

My dad would also come into my bedroom in the middle of the night and get in bed with me. He would hold me tight all through the night in spoon fashion with his genitals up against my buttocks. He told me not to move. I was unable to move and could not sleep the whole night.

During this time, I may have touched his genital area more than once. I definitely recall the one time that I did this.

My father was also physically and verbally abusive. There were times when he would call me "a God damn stupid idiot." He would also beat me for reasons that I could not understand. He would take me into a very small closet and make me strip down naked and beat me violently with a belt. I was afraid he would hit me in the head with the belt buckle and would kill me. I could not get away. I can still remember the smell of tobacco on his clothes in the closet.

My mother would then put lotion on my welts and tell me, "Your father loves you very much." This was very confusing to me.

Once I kissed my dad on the head at a football game just to show him a sign of affection.

He slapped me in the face and told me, "Men don't kiss!"

When my mother was away, my father would also ask me to massage his back and naked buttocks with lotion and massage near his anus. I was only 11 at the time, but already having same-sex feelings. I would get aroused when doing this.

My mother other was also emotionally and covertly sexually abusive. She would give me enemas a lot as a kid and teenager. I am not sure why she did that. She would take me into the bathroom, lock the door, and have me lay down on the floor. She would pull down my underwear and insert Vaseline in my rectum with her finger and then insert the nozzle. It was very arousing. When she was done, she would ask me to turn over. I had an erection and did not want her to see it. This behavior started around the age of 3 and continued until the age of 15. I developed an enema fetish in my 30's.

My mother had no boundaries. She would sit naked in her bedroom and put on her makeup while talking to me.

She would also ask me to come into the bathroom when she was taking a bath and was douching herself. I found this very disturbing and icky.

She would also confide in me that she and my father did not have a very good relationship, she told me that their sex life was not very satisfying. She told me that she was happy that she could confide in me. I became her emotional caretaker and surrogate spouse. She told me that I was very special to her.

My older brother was sexually abusive. He would play doctor with me. He later told me that he thought maybe his behavior caused me to be gay. In later life, he would not tell me what we did when we played doctor. This all occurred before the age of 11 because that was when he moved out of the house. He is very upset today that I am gay and believes that Jesus can save me from this sin. When I shared with him the abuse a few years ago, he told me that he had no empathy because I was looking to blame. He told me our dad was always a man to him. And the fondling of my testicles was just because my dad was curious and had hopes to be a doctor and was interested in anatomy. My dad also had an enema fetish. He would lay naked and take the enema and then leave the equipment hanging over the bathtub. My brother said that my father did this because he was allergic to milk and that was why he took enemas.

My older brother also experienced the trauma of our dysfunctional system. When my father was still active in his alcoholism, my brother had to go into bars to get him. He also saw my father sitting on the porch one night with a gun to his head. There was also a time when my father threatened to jump off a tall building with my brother and mother present.

My older brother has raised two wonderful children. He is a faithful Christian man. He has visited the sick, fed the hungry and witnessed to his faith. He is a very talented artist. He He has given me two lovely pieces of artwork.

My sister is the only one in the family who did not abuse me sexually. She taught me how to dance and often invited me to parties with her friends. She made my twin and I the mascots of her high school pep club. She took care of me and would often cook for me when my mother was at work. She teases me that whenever she asked my twin and I what we would like for breakfast, that we always asked for "French Toast." I have shared the abuse with her. She has done many kind and wonderful things for me.

After having experienced sex with my twin and other boys, I was very confused and ashamed. To top that off my peers whom I had known since elementary school found out that I was gay. They all rejected me. I would go to sit down at a table with my peers in the cafeteria and everyone at the table would get up and move to another table. I usually ate alone. The only exception was when some of the older girls at school would drive me to a great hamburger joint during the lunch hour. I loved those girls.

There was a boy in my school who wanted me to orally service him. I asked him if he would the same to me. He exclaimed, *"NO!"*

I told him that I would not service him if he didn't do the same for me. When I said "No," he got really pissed off. After that, he would follow me home from school, slap me on the head, and yell, "God don't make *FAGS!"*

This boy wanted to set a time to fight me. I told my dad that this boy wanted to fight. Of course, I did not tell him the reason why. He said that I should face him like a man. He sent my twin to play referee. The boy had very long arms and was able to hit me much easier than I could hit him. He gave me two black eyes.

The next day when I went to school people asked me what happened. I told them that I ran into a door. I wished my father had gone to the fight and stood up for me.

At the age of 15, I became very depressed and suicidal. I actually took the razor blade out of the medicine cabinet when I was 15 to cut my wrists, but decided to talk to a youth minister who talked me out of committing suicide. I am glad that he did.

I was feeling very much alone, guilty, and ashamed. I heard in Sunday school from our teacher that homosexuality was wrong. This same teacher's son molested me in the gym bathroom when there was a break from our church basketball team practice. He was so handsome and I really liked the attention. He also had an enema fetish so I did not feel so alone in this practice. I desperately wanted his friendship, but he groomed me and used me for his own sexual needs. He would always tell me not tell anybody about my performing oral sex on him.

The father of the boy who molested and groomed me was my Sunday School teacher at church. He would teach us that homosexuality was wrong and a sin. Later that year, the church school teacher's wife divorced him because he was having an affair with another woman. The youngest of the church school teacher's son later came out as gay.

Wanting to escape the pain and reality of my situation, I left a note under my mother's pillow telling her that I was having sex with my twin and other boys. I told her that I was in so much pain but I did not want to kill myself. I needed help and understanding. After I put the note under her pillow, I decided that I would run away. My mother used to tease me that if I ever wanted to leave she would pack me a lunch. I got as far as the park in my neighborhood, and then realized I had nowhere to go. I returned home. My mother had not found the note. So she had me read it to her.

After reading it, I think that she said that I was just going through a phase but I assured her that it was not a phase and that I was in a lot of pain. She said she would tell my father, but she was afraid that the news that I was gay might drive him back to active alcoholism.

My father made "appointments" with my twin and I in a room in our home. He told me that he was proud of me for my honesty. That he would get me help. He would send my twin and I to his psychiatrist. My father told me that he could understand people having sex with women or animals, but never with a man.

I went to meet with the psychiatrist. This psychiatrist utilized shock treatment and I was so afraid he would use it on me. I told him that I was in a lot of pain and I began to cry. I hoped he would understand and could help me. This overweight, cigar-smoking man told me that I should feel guilty because homosexuality was wrong. He told me that he would give me tranquilizers to help me cut down on my compulsive masturbation. He told me to look at girlie magazines and masturbate. He also suggested that I fantasize about my girlfriend when masturbating. This was very confusing as he gave me the tranquilizers to cut down on the masturbation. He asked my mother to come and have a session with him, but she did not want to talk to him. She told me that he would blame her for my being gay.

The therapist did not deal with the incest nor the family abuse. At the time I did not know it was abuse.

When you are in a closed family system you just think that this is the way families behave. My twin and I became the "identifying patients." The dysfunctional system finds someone to blame. I carried the burden of expectation that if my behavior changed, the whole family would be happy. Earlier, I had thought that if I committed suicide the family would no longer have this "bad seed."

The therapist wanted me to be straight. I decided that I would be the person everyone wanted me to be.

I asked the prettiest girls in my high school for dates. I started going steady with a girl who was in my theater class and in plays. My dad did not like her because she was Catholic and wore too much makeup. We broke up just before she and I left to attend different colleges.

From this time on, I limited my sexual behavior to fantasy and masturbation to male images in magazines. I was terrified of having any sexual contacts with another human being. I did not have any sexual relationships until my late 20's, years after college.

Jerry as American Gothic Man (the farmer) in the SAG movie, I Heart Shakey, 2012

Jerry as Tin Man in The Wizard of Oz, Greer Garson Theatre, Santa Fe, New Mexico, 1995

ALCOHOLISM

I had my first drink when I was around 12 or 13. My dad, who was a recovering alcoholic, came into my room one evening with a beautiful box. He told me that he had something for me. He opened the box and there was a premium bottle of whiskey. There were two shot glasses in the box and he poured me one and asked me to drink it. It burned, but I liked the effect. I asked him if I could have another one and he laughed. My father got sober from alcohol in a 12-Step when I was 3 years old.

I drank beer in college and one night my best friend and I got in trouble by driving his pick-up truck across the greens of the college golf course.

I drank with fraternity brothers, but I never got drunk.

My mom hosted parties when I would return home on occasional weekends from the college that I was attending. She would make and serve strawberry daiquiris to me and my friends.

When my twin and I were in college, we worked summers at a Lodge by a beautiful lake in Minnesota. We worked as bellhops. My twin wrote a comedy skit that we performed in the evenings for the tourists staying at the lodge. The tourists loved it. We both drank heavily every night after work at the lodge. At the end of the summer we drove back on the Kansas City Turnpike to our Midwestern city of upbringing before returning to college.

We still had several bottles of liquor in the backseat of the car that were left from our summer partying. We were not drinking, but were still suffering the effects of binging the previous night. One of the tires on the car was starting to go flat. We stopped at a filling station. We could not afford a new tire, but the filling station attendant offered to temporarily repair it at no charge. He said the temporary fix will enable us to get to our destination problem-free.

The speed limit on the highway was 80 mph. It started to rain. The car began to hydroplane. We slid into the grassy median strip separating the opposing lanes of traffic.

The car continued to rise up the other side of the median to the other side of the highway where the cars were going in the opposite direction. We were hit on the side by a car going 80 mph. I was sitting on the right side. I saw it coming and thought that this was the end.

The man driving suffered a broken nose as the result of the accident. His wife and daughter were in the car with him, but they were not harmed. I was in shock. Jim and I had minor cuts and bruises. My father bought us plane tickets to get us home. The car was totaled.

Not having money to fix the tire, we spent our money to drink, senses dulled by the drinking causing delayed response time—a combination of all these "may have" created the accident.

My drinking began to increase when I was in theology school. Fellow students and I would go to the lake near the campus with bread and wine. I usually got drunk. The hangovers were awful. I usually had severe headaches and nausea.

I also used to join my fellow grad students for beer and peanuts at a local bar. We would drink several pitchers and discuss theology.

After graduate school, I would buy bottles of beer at gay bars and lose count of how many I had. I would get drunk. I usually stopped at a Jack in the Box to get some tacos before getting home.

I would eat them at home sitting in the living room chair. I would get mustard and ketchup all over my shirt. I went to bed with one foot on the floor to keep the room from spinning and to keep me from throwing up.

My first job out of theology school was managing an innovative, arts, recreation and educational center in a very affluent neighborhood in a large city in Texas.

Part of the program was to provide after school activities for latchkey kids who were heavily involved in drug use. I was trying to help with their drug use, but I was still drinking heavily.

My job ended after the minister who created the program died. His replacement was not interested in innovative programs.

I started waiting tables and bartending. I got drunk every evening. I stayed up until the early morning hours partying with employees. We would gamble by playing liar's poker, drink, smoke marijuana, go out for food, and crash at someone's house. Almost all of the tips that I made from waiting tables and bartending were spent on partying. I remember very sincerely asking one of the waitresses at the restaurant if she thought my life would ever amount to anything.

One night while at work at the restaurant, my mom called to tell me that my father would probably not live through the night. He had cancer of the spleen. The cancer was spreading throughout his body. Removing the spleen by surgery was not an option in the late 70's and the chemotherapy was not successful in eradicating it. I took a flight out the next morning.

I was not really there for my dad during his sickness and eventual death. I was more concerned about my own life and was depressed about my own future. After work, I even spent the night before the flight getting drunk and skinny-dipping with employees.

I was appointed to my first local church in a small Texas town after theology school. On the weekends, I would drive to a larger city about 45 minutes away, visit the gay bars, and drink heavily.

One night, while driving back to the small town where I lived, I had a blackout. When I awoke, I was veering off the country road and I turned the car wheel hard to the left. The car went of control and began to roll. The car made two complete revolutions and then came to a halt on the muddy bed off the side of the road.

The highway patrol that came along told me that I smelled like a brewery. They said that a policeman would be along to deal with the matter as it was outside their jurisdiction. I told the policeman who arrived next that I had a couple of drinks to relax from the demanding and stressful job of ministry. The policeman told me that his job was stressful, too, and he understood. He did not give me a DWI.

The music and choir director at the church I served in the small town told members of the congregation that not only had I wrecked my car because I had been drinking, but that I also had youth in the car with me. That latter part was not true. I was by myself.

A congregational meeting was called to talk about the incident. The coach of the women's track team who was a close friend stood up during the discussion and said, "If we are going to fire Jerry for having a few drinks, then half of this congregation should be fired." There was resounding applause. An entire congregation enabled me. I manipulated members of the congregation to get the musical director fired.

As I continued in ministry, I promised myself that I would only go to the gay bars on weekends. I ended up going to the bars almost every night and getting drunk.

I finally left the church when the senior minister refused to support me in "coming out" to the congregation. He said that he loved me and supported me, but he had a wife and children to support and would not risk losing his job.

I continued to go to gay bars and get drunk. I asked a friend in the city if I could stay at his place until I sobered up. I was still driving drunk to his place.

There were many times when I was drunk when I came home or elsewhere with someone from the bars and woke up wondering where I was and how I got there.

There was a time when I worked as a bartender at a downtown bar visited by young corporate businessmen. As soon as I closed the bar, I would go to a gay bar and get drunk. I would drive back to a place in the country where I was staying. I was living with a friend in a small farmhouse that he was repairing. The house had no heat. The toilet did not work unless you put antifreeze in it to keep it from freezing. I had no bed–just an old down filled cocoon style sleeping bag. I shook violently from the cold until my body started to get warm in the sleeping bag.

Eventually, I was hired for campus ministry at a community college in a suburb near Dallas. I still drank, but I enjoyed my job. I brought in well-known guest speakers, helped to start a program where students could get academic credit for volunteering in social service agencies, taught a class on vocational guidance, and started an Institute for Life Long Learning. I wrote a course book at this time.

I was happy with my job, but I was still drinking in the evenings. I would always have the jitters the next day.

My dad used to take me to 12-Step meetings at a club when I was a kid. I remembered the attention and kindness the people in recovery showed me, There were holiday parties and dances. I remember the smell of coffee and the streams of cigarette smoke billowing through the rooms.

There was a Dairy Queen close to where I lived in Dallas. I often went there for lunch. It was located in a shopping complex. As I ate, I would look outside the window and see a door that had the slogan "One Day At A Time." I knew it was a 12-Step meeting for alcoholics, but I wrestled with whether or not I was an alcoholic. I really battled inside–should I accept and surrender or stay in denial.

One night, I was outside a gay bar when I noticed a friend outside. He seemed really happy. He told me that he had stopped drinking and was going to a 12-Step meeting. He said it was a gay group. I told him that I knew about this 12-Step program as my father was a recovering alcoholic. I said that I didn't really drink that much but sometimes overdid it. He invited me to a meeting.

A straight man was giving the lead and I was not able to identify. At the meeting, desire chips were offered for those who had a desire to stop drinking. I hesitated. The guy behind me pushed me out of my chair and told me to go get a desire chip. After the meeting, everyone joined hands and said The Lord's Prayer. I was moved that a group of gay men were holding hands and praying.

After the meeting, two people that I recognized invited me to have coffee with them.

As I drank coffee with them, I told them that I probably would not come back as it would offend those who really had a problem with alcoholism. They suggested that I experiment to see if I was an alcoholic. They told me to go to a bar and have one drink. They told me to go the next night and have one drink.

I told them, "I can't do that."

They told me that maybe I needed to keep coming back. I came back to the meetings.

I have stayed continually sober from alcohol and drugs since August 20, 1980.

GAMBLING

My mother took me to Vegas when I was in college. I won $100 dollars in the slot machine.

This was when my gambling addiction started. My mom took me on many trips to Vegas. I would lose all my winnings and borrow money from her. At first, I lost about $300. Later in my gambling addiction I lost $1,000 at the crap table on every trip. In graduate school, while working on my MFA I went and played video gaming machines after classes. I lost about $300 each time.

My dad also took me to the horse races. He limited himself to $50 dollars per trip. I always went over my limit of $50 dollars. I also started going with my sister to dog races and later to casinos in Colorado where she lived and I always lost.

I also played poker or gin rummy with my family for dimes and quarters. I played poker with friends for money. I also played liar's poker with friends and cheated many times.

One time, I was attending a 12-Step convention in Las Vegas. I wrestled with whether to go to the convention's dinner events or gamble. I gambled and lost about $2,000. My mom, my twin brother and my sister joined me in Vegas after the convention. I borrowed money from my mother and lost another $2,000.

I decided to attend a 12-Step meeting for gambling. I now no longer gamble large sums. I buy an occasional lottery ticket or play bingo at my residence for prizes. That is now the extent of my gambling.

By the end of my gambling, I had racked up about $18,000 in gambling debts. It was my mother who bailed me out.

Jerry as a farmer on an interstate billboard for the New Mexico State Fair. He also appeared in a television commercial for the Fair, 2000

Jerry as Gramps in Arthur Miller's American Clock, Redtwist Theatre, Chicago, 2015

ACTING OUT

I was ironically in graduate school for theology in Dallas when I went to my first gay bar. The school had various field trips. One of them was to a gay bar. The purpose was to desensitize students to persons in the LGBTQ community. It was the field trip to a gay bar that introduced me to the gay scene. Good or bad, the feeling of being alone dissipated, thanks to that trip.

I started going to the bars and meeting other gay men. Initially, I went home with people, had sex, and as soon as the sex was over, I raced out of their places. I felt fear, guilt and shame. I just could never be present after the sex. Those trysts were quick moments. On occasion, I spent the night. As I became more comfortable with my sexuality, I was able to date and spend more time with someone and enjoyed spending the night.

I don't believe going to gay bars made one sexually compulsive. In my late 20s during the '70s, in Dallas, Texas where I lived, one could not be open about one's sexuality.

You had to go underground. You became a member of a subculture. To be open was dangerous. You could lose your job just for being gay regardless of you competency. Police often raided bars and turned the lights on over the dance floor. If they spied men demonstrating affection with another man, they arrested them. There were also drive-by shootings.

Men who cruised parks for sex were often kidnapped and forced at gunpoint to withdraw large amounts of money from their accounts. The kidnappers then killed the gay man. There was one horrible incident I still vividly remember.

Two college students from a conservative religious suburb picked up a young man who was outside a gay bar. They took him to a park and put a gun to his head. They forced him to perform oral sex on both of them. Then they shot him in the head and killed him. The two college students were later arrested. At their hearing, the judge let them off. He ruled that they had been enticed.

The gay bars served a purpose. You could be openly gay with hundreds of other men. You could dance with other men and have fun. You could go home with someone and receive affection and enjoy your sexuality. In many ways it was wonderful.

There was also a downside. Major liquor companies hosted events at the bars.

Alcohol, and drugs as well, were and continue to be,

a prominent feature of the bars. I think, for many of us, they are ways of numbing out internally the external homophobia from so many voices that tell us that we are bad, depraved, sinners and psychological aberrations.

My goal for being at a bar then was to go home with someone before the bar closed. My self-esteem got enhanced when someone found me attractive and wanted to have sex with me. I really enjoyed those times.

When no one wanted to go home with me, I went into deep depression. This fueled my alcoholism. Maybe, I really longed for a relationship, but there were no avenues for dating, social events nor church events. I did ask men for dates and some agreed. We went out for dinner and then had sex, but there was rarely a second date.

It was sad to go to a bar and see someone you had dated or had sex with looking for someone else besides you.

I entered therapy. I had initial appointments with two psychologists and one counselor.

One psychologist told me that there was nothing wrong about being gay. That scared me.

The other psychologist told me that we needed to explore my heterosexuality first.

The counselor in theology school told me that if I were gay, it would be better not to proceed into the ministry. He felt that it would be too difficult a journey for me.

I chose the therapist that encouraged me to explore

my heterosexuality.

I dated women and finally had a sexual experience with a woman. We both smoked and drank a lot. I didn't really like her, but I wanted to become a "man."

So it happened one night. I was so anxious. I had a quick orgasm. Later, this woman told me she thought she was pregnant. I told her that she had to get an abortion.

I dated other women. I asked one woman to marry me. She declined. I was sexually active during this time with both men and women. My sex addiction told me that sex was my most important need. My addiction progressed.

I later got a "full-body" massage from a masseur. He brought me to orgasm. It was such a high. I continued to visit full-body masseurs. I also bought prostitutes. I came up with a way to get money to spend on the masseurs and prostitutes. I started giving full-body massages to men myself for money. Oftentimes, this turned into my own prostitution. I used clients who thought they were in love with me.

I had sex with four co-workers.

I also tried to seduce others while we were both drunk. Once, I forcibly masturbated a good friend when we were drunk.

All this escalated. I engaged in compulsive masturbation, anonymous sex, paying and being paid for sex and more perverted fetishism.

I was spending around $250 a week on prostitutes.

The full body massages, the forcible masturbation, the fetish, the paying young men for sex, all these were related to the sexual abuse. All these repeated over and over, again and again.

I was unable to define and separate love, sex and affection. My skewed thinking equated sex as containing all three.

I wanted desperately to be loved and sought to find love through sex.

I even tried to become friends with the male sex workers I hired.

My last "acting out" was with an 18-year old male prostitute.

I started to attend several 12-Step sexual addiction recovery groups. I stayed sober for a year or two, but I always relapsed with full body massages.

It wasn't until I participated in 12-Step groups that practiced abstinence until married or abstinence outside a mutually exclusive relationship that I gained long term sobriety.

My sexuality is now enhanced and fulfilling because I am in a monogamous relationship with someone I love and continue to grow in love with.

My sex addiction began when I was 11 years old. Compulsive sex consumed all my time and energy. My sex addiction was my best friend. I isolated myself. I let go of friends and events because I might miss out on a sexual high. I was tortured by loneliness. I was filled with self-hate. My focus was on what I could get rather than what I could give. I harmed people and let others harm me. I became willing to fetishes, to do activities that were not normal even for me.

I went through all this, but knew I had to commit myself 100% to getting sober. I have been sober from my sex addiction since May 26, 2010.

As a result, my emotional, spiritual, financial, social and creative selves have all expanded and changed for the better.

Sobriety is a process. I was willing, sometimes reluctantly and defiantly, to do what others who had achieved long term sobriety did. I worked the 12-Step, called my sponsor everyday, worked with others, prayed and meditated and went to meetings.

In my mind, I still consider myself not fully recovered. I will always be an addict, but I also tell myself that I don't have to be active in my addictions. I have a daily reprieve from addiction as I continue to practice the principles of the 12-Steps in all my affairs and turn my will and my life over to the care of a Higher Power daily.

MY BEST FRIEND

- *Jerry*

Homemade fried chicken, mashed potatoes,

and corn on the cob.

Table set just right.

Cherry pie to end the night. Christmas

goodies made from scratch.

Divinity, fudge, fruit cake, pralines you

could not match. Leader of PTA,

Den Mother,

Church camp sponsor, Party giver,

Chauffeured and delivered.

Brought to a church where I could dance,

Baptized, prayed for,

and love of Jesus taught to enhance,

the journey of faith that she could

demonstrate. Showed where to go if

alcohol became a foe.

Loved always wherever I would go. To the
depths or height,
Always sent and returned with light of love.
Sad to lose my best friend.
Who told me to take it "one day at a time."
And everything would be just fine.
Still likes ice cream at 97, Getting ready to
go to heaven. Always grateful to the end.
Fought the good fight with all her might.
God watch over my mom tonight.

**Jerry as Bottom, A Midsummer Night's Dream,
Santa Fe Shakespeare, New Mexico, July 1989**

Jerry as Salvation Army team member, Guys and Dolls, Light Opera Works, Evanston, Illinois, 2015

FORGIVING MY MOM

I was able to be with my dying mother during her last three months on earth. I prayed with her, sang to her, talked to her. She told me that she wanted to make amends for any mistakes she made. She said that she wanted me to be happy and do what I loved doing.

I believe that this sacred period happened because I confronted my mother about her own abuse of me about 20 years beforehand. I told her that I was "goddamn angry" that she abused me with enemas and did not protect me from my father's beatings. I got the anger out. Back then, I was also in recovery.

On her last months, I also made amends to her for not being the son I could have been. I used her to bail me out of gambling debts and borrowed money because I was spending it on massages and prostitutes. I was not fully available to her because of my addictions.

Mother had attended alanon meetings herself and

Jerry as Prince, Renaissance Faire, Mesquite, Texas, 1977

practiced the principles of that program when my father was recovering from alcoholism.

On one of the last few days before her death, she said, "You know what we do?"

I asked, "What?"

She answered, "We take it just one day at a time."

My mom had her shortcomings, but so do I. Her mom and sister died when she was very young. This does not absolve her from the abuse, but she made her amends.

I will still claim that she gave me the better values that I now carry. She was outgoing and never knew a stranger. She always continued to grow and change. She learned how to use a computer in her 70's. She traveled the world and often took me with her. She married three times. Three men dearly loved her. She remarried because she outlived her husbands.

She opened her house to my friends and welcomed them always. She became an advocate for people with HIV/AIDS. She donated paintings for auctions to raise money for people living with AIDS. She worked most of her life at wonderful jobs even though she never finished college.

She was a great cook. On a recent Christmas season, I got her recipe box out—the one that my sister gave me. I made Christmas Candy from her recipes for the first time. It was a wonderful time for memories and gratitude for my mom.

**Jerry as Lord Capulet in Romeo and Juliet, Glass
Onion Theatre, Chicago, 2011**

MY TWIN JIM

I cannot tell you now when my twin forcibly started to masturbate me, but this continued until we were 18. I was repulsed by the thought, yet I enjoyed the pleasure.

You could say that, in a way, I used him as well. One time, when he was visiting me, he told me that he wouldn't have abused me if he had not been abused himself.

I am grateful for my twin. We are close. We can share our recovery, we were able collaborate on this book. We can share our stories with each other and with others. We share the joy of being alive.

Jerry as Bottom, A Midsummer Night's Dream, Santa Fe Shakespeare, New Mexico, July 1989

HEALTH

I believe that sobriety helps to create good health and resilience from illness and health complications. When I was active in my addictions, I did not practice a healthy lifestyle. It was a self-destructive path.

I do have Chronic Obstructive Pulmonary Disease (COPD) caused by smoking for 39 years. I gave up my nicotine addiction over 20 years ago. My COPD does not limit my activities. It is now kept in check by medication.

I gave up my car and take public transportation.

I walk about 3 to 5 miles everyday. I recently had laparoscopic colorectal surgery for a large polyp, but it was benign. The surgeons were amazed at how quickly I recovered. During the surgery and afterward, I felt that God was present and taking care of me. Loving friends came to see me.

I take proactive steps to maintain my health. I have lost 30 pounds from a low-carb diet. I still struggle with caffeine. Still, after a recent lipid test from an overnight stay in the hospital, one of the doctors who was about 35 years old said that my lipids were better than his.

If I were still drinking, consuming large amounts of sugar, smoking, and overweight, I would in all likelihood be dead by now. The stress of addictions really does damage on the mind, soul, emotions and body.

I think that as I feel better about myself, I want to take care of myself more.

I am learning to love myself.

FORBIDDEN FRUIT

- *Jerry*

That's what I was. Forbidden Fruit,

A fruit forbidden from being included,

   Spoiled Fruit

Rotten to the Core. Smelling to high heaven.

   Damaged goods.

Soured, green, red faced. Dropped.

Laying on the ground, tarnished, abandoned.

   Not any good for all-American pie.

That's what I am. Forbidden Fruit

But today I am ripe for picking.

Picked up and laid on the ground by firm

   hands which are drawn to my pungent

   aroma

For forbidden pleasure.

Heavenly sap emanating from that which is

   hard and red, Filled with seeds emerging

from pulpy flesh that touch

my core.

Eaten in the Garden of Eden.

The eve of ripening from pulpy flesh that

touch my core. Eaten in the Garden of

Eden.

The eve of ripening from green to fiery red.

The forbidden deed. Done.

The apple in someone's eye.

HEALTHY LOVE

I am now in a healthy, emotional, spiritual, sexual relationship with another man.

We have been partners for over two years. He is caring, respectful, generous, and loving. As I write this, in the early fall of 2017, we will be getting engaged in December of 2017.

I believe there are many reasons that this healthy relationship has happened.

I was sober from sex addiction and abstinent for 7 years. I worked the 12-Steps in several fellowships.

I wrote a dating plan. I defined what type of man I wanted to be in a relationship with.

We courted for five months before becoming sexually intimate. I set boundaries about affection during the courting. We limited our affection to simple kisses, hugs, and holding hands.

We did a variety of things together in different environments. We had coffee and had long talks. We went bowling, out to movies, out for dinners. We attended events with mutual friends.

The Bible has a term for sexual intimacy. It is called "being known."

We have taken a long time to get to know one another. It is a continual process, and we have become so comfortable in talking about all areas of our lives. We can express our needs to one another.

We also share an interest in theater. We share a spiritual path and we often attend church together.

We have a monogamous, mutually exclusive relationship. It is such a joy to have a fellow gay male companion. We have a lot of fun. We go on short trips when he has work in New York or in other parts of the United States. We enjoy cooking for one another. We live just a few blocks from each other. We are accountable to each other. I am committed to this relationship.

I believe this relationship is a gift from God.

LETTING MY LIGHT SHINE

I once read the narration of a Christmas Pageant in elementary school. I loved doing this. The spotlight was just on me. I discovered that I could move people with words from scripture and contemporary prose.

My heart was warmed. I was encouraged. After the Christmas Pageant, people came up and congratulated me.

My mom used to say, "just tell them that it is a gift from God." I used to wonder why I should tell people that when it was I who worked pretty hard to be good "moving people," yet she had always been right.

I took elocution lessons from a lady and practiced memorizing stories and poems. One of my favorites was The Creation by James Weldon Johnson.

In my teenage years, I was cast in plays at church, at theaters and in school.

I won the Junior High Drama Award and the Senior

High Drama Award.

Once, I told my father that I wanted to pursue acting as soon as I graduated from 12th grade.

He told me, "Son, you don't want to be an actor. All actors are gay!"

I wanted to reply, "What about John Wayne?" He was one of my father's favorite movie stars. I decided not to. I didn't tell him that I was "gay" either.

I instead went to college and studied to be a minister. I was active in my church. My dad really appreciated me pursuing the ministerial path. I didn't have much self-esteem at the time. I had doubts about whether I could really be a good actor.

I continued to act in smaller community plays. Sometimes, I performed at the church plays where I also served.

After 19 years in ministry, I decided to move to a southwestern city and open an antique shop and art gallery with my mother and my sister. I worked in the shop for $5 an hour while I studied acting and performed in plays. My goal was to be in a movie, do major roles on stage, become a member of Screen Actors Guild and be in a commercial. I accomplished all this in this southwestern city.

After five years of honing my craft, I decided to apply at a professional school for acting. A the age of 50, I decided that I wanted to obtain a Masters in Fine Arts in Acting. I wanted to follow the dream of my heart.

I was accepted at a university in the south. I was voted Outstanding MFA actor by the faculty and board of the theater department. I was also the first actor from my graduate school to be chosen for a year long paid internship at a prestigious theater in the Midwest. I understudied major roles and had small roles.

After the internship I became a member of Actors Equity, the union for professional actors.

Then I moved to Chicago, a city that is rated #3 in terms of its film and stage opportunities for actors. I lived with three other actors on the second floor of an apartment complex. I had a very small room with no air conditioning. The air conditioner was in the living room. The summer that I moved there was the hottest on record. Many seniors died from the heat that year.

All three of us slept in the living room where the air conditioner was.

I auditioned for plays. I signed with a talent agent. I worked catering and hosting jobs.

I really struggled to eat and pay my bills. I took buses and subways to many catering jobs because I could not afford a taxi.

I finally got my first professional acting job in an

Equity theatre. It paid $125 a week. I was so excited. The play received great reviews. My job at the time did not pay the bills, so to make more money, I worked in the corporate world as an executive assistant. I still performed in plays in the evenings.

At the age of 60, I started taking voice lessons so I could audition for musicals.

I have now been working steadily as an actor. I recently did a commercial and had a small speaking part in a SAG movie.

I have appeared in many singing roles for a musical theatre company the employs a 26-piece union orchestra for its shows. I have produced and sung in a gay cabaret with actors and professional singers to raise money for a homeless shelter.

I have written and produced two of my plays. I have written a book, ***Empty Space: Creating A Theatre in Your Church Step-by-Step,*** about how I started four theaters in local churches to educate, motivate and activate audiences to do social justice, and how others can do this as well.

I have had productions which raised money for non-profits to build wells and teach English in South Sudan, raised money for organizations that assist people living with AIDS and helped fund church budgets.

I started a Filipino youth juggling troupe that performs all over the state of Illinois.

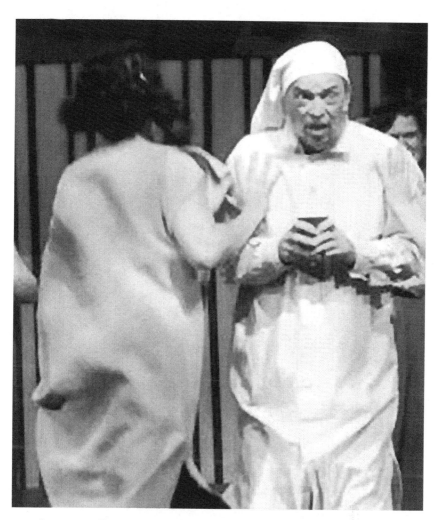

Jerry as Scrooge in A Christmas Carol, Metropolis Performing Arts Centre, 2013

Harding High School won the sweepstakes and one-act play trophies and Jerry Miller, 1200 NW 37, who had the lead role in the play, shows them off.

Jerry featured in the main Oklahoma City newspaper holding two trophies, one for his high school winning a sweepstakes and another for a one-act play in which he starred as the co-lead actor. Oklahoma City, Oklahoma, 1962

I have also produced and co-directed a variety of musicals and plays.

As I write this in 2017, I have appeared in the musical Gypsy, I will be playing Scrooge in A Christmas Carol at a prominent theater in the suburbs. I have also been cast in a major role in the musical, Grand Hotel, in Chicago.

I am very happy that I can do what my heart loves.

My mom gave me a poster once with a quote from Langston Hughes:

> *Hold fast to dreams*
> *For if dreams die*
> *Life is a broken-winged bird*
> *That cannot fly.*
>
> *Hold fast to dreams*
> *For when dreams go*
> *Life is a barren field*
> *Frozen with snow.*

My higher power, which I choose to call God, has rocketed me into another dimension. I try and keep in conscious contact with this Power. I try to see what I can bring to others. I admit when I am wrong and seek to change my direction. I have made amends with those I had harmed in my addictions and I am willing to make amends with those I am unable to find at this moment.

It has been said that "no matter how far down the scale we have gone, we can see how our experience can benefit others."

I am writing this tell-all book of my worst trials and grateful recovery because I am honored to share my experience, strength and hope with others who are also recovering from addictions. This is my greatest gift from God.

There is light in my life and the darkness will never put it out. I feel like that innocent child who loves this big beautiful world.

Happy, Joyous and Free.

Preparing for first take as county clerk in the television series, Lucky Luke, 1990s

Jerry fishing with dad in Colorado when he was 13 years old, 1958

DEAR DAD

Dear Dad,

I am writing you a letter to make amends with you.

I was not the kind of son that I could have been.

You told me at one of our last visits that you had done another 4th step in a 12-Step group, and that you wanted to make amends for not being the father that you could have been.

At the time, I was in the throes of my alcoholism, and I really was not able to hear you nor have a good conversation with you about that. I was not fully conscious of the physical, emotional nor sexual abuses that were part of our relationship until later in life.

I forgive you because I know that you must have gone through incredible pain when you were a child yourself at the hands of your father.

I regret that you are not alive today so healing could

take place in our relationship. You were on a healing path then, but I was not. I feel very sad about that.

I want you to know that I am happy. That I am sober and life is good. I am doing what I have always wanted to do, being an actor, director and producer.

I know that you would have preferred that I stayed a minister. I still preach occasionally and officiate weddings for straight and gay couples.

And I am sober, thanks to what you shared in the past about your own recovery journeys.

You once told me that you were religious and spiritual, but not like Anita Bryant. I don't know if you were joking or serious, but this made it a lot easier for me to accept being gay. I felt that you meant you just wanted me to be happy.

I would not have the love of fishing nor have become a great fisherman without you teaching me.

I did mom's funeral in Oklahoma City. She loved you and wanted to be next to you. I went to the gravesite to tell you that I forgive you.

When you were dying, I was still drinking. I could have been more present for you, shared my love and cared for you. I ask for your forgiveness for that. I was selfish and self-centered. I felt relief when you died because we never formed a good relationship. Had I been sober then, I think we could have worked on improving our communication

Jerry getting ready to go on as Cigar in the musical, Gypsy, Music Theatre Works, 2017

and love for one another.

I know that you helped a lot of people recover from alcoholism. As soon as you discovered that you had cancer, you became more active in your 12-Step recovery. In your last years, you started delivering meals for Meals on Wheels and started sponsoring people again. You dedicated yourself to being about love and service.

Addiction really destroys lives. I am glad that you remained sober for over 35 years and that you died sober. That was your real gift to me.

Thank your for all the material things you gave me. Thank you for an education, fine clothes, a car, trips. Thank you for the experiences such as the World's Fair, going fishing with me, coming to all my graduations, paying for my trip to Europe.

I am sorry that I was unable to give back to you.

I don't know if there is a heaven. If there is, we will both be there to embrace each other with open arms.

Forgive my judgments and criticisms of you.

I guess my greatest gift that I can give back to you is to stay sober, be happy and be open to help others.

I owe you my life.

Your son,
Jerry

Before and After. Jerry with a beard, Jim clean shaven. Taking a picture to fool people that it's the same person, 1973

ABUSED. ADDICTED.
ALIVE!

THE DAY
THE RAIN
CAME DOWN

THE END

ABOUT THE AUTHORS

JAMES F. MILLER

James F. Miller is the identical twin brother of Jerry M. Miller, a Chicago actor, producer and director.

A former Chicagoan himself, James has been writing for most of his life. He was an Oklahoma Junior Writer of the Year at age 17 and published his first book of poetry when he was 15 years old called *Life, Death and Man Between.*

Neon Lights is his second published book of poetry. It tells his journey as a gay man with stories of abuse and love.

His poetry and short stories have been published in several anthologies and magazines.

Mr. Miller was a feature story writer for the Chicago Tribune and the Chicago Sun Times.

He studied for his masters at Madill School of Journalism at Northwestern University.

He holds a Bachelor of the Arts degree in Journalism from the University of Oklahoma, a Masters in English from Central State in Edmond, Oklahoma and a Masters in Education from the University of Phoenix.

He recently studied screenwriting at Colorado College in Colorado Springs, Colorado and has written his first screenplay about a lesbian couple and their children.

Mr. Miller is also a professional artist and his work has been shown and sold in juried shows.

JERRY M. MILLER

Jerry M. Miller is a Chicago actor, theater producer, director, playwright, and author. This is Jerry's secondbook. His previous work, **Empty Space: Creating A Theater in Your Church Step-by-Step** is available from Amazon or from the author. The book advocates doing theater to teach, activate, and motivate audiences to do social justice.

Jerry created four theaters in churches in the Chicago Area. The book has been given favorable Amazon reviews by noted authors Bishop Joseph Sprague, Mel White, and Tex Sample.

Jerry earned an MFA in acting from the University of South Carolina and received "Outstanding MFA Acting Candidate" by the faculty and board. Jerry spent a one year internship at the Milwaukee Repertory Theater as the male lead understudy and actor.

Jerry is a member of Screen Actors Guild (SAG) and

(EMC) complete for Actor's Equity. Jerry has been seen in roles at Writers Theatre, Music Theater Works, Red Twist Theatre, Theater Wit, Walkabout Theater, and Metropolis Performing Arts in the Chicago area.

Jerry received an MTH in Theology from Perkins School of Theology at SMU in Dallas. He is a retired ordained openly gay United Methodist Minister.

Jerry is passionate about social justice. His play, *The Long Walk for Water,* was adapted from the children's New York Times Best Seller book, *A Long Walk to Water* by Linda Sue Park, Houghton Mifflin Court. Jerry's play helped to raise $18,000 for nonprofits to build wells for villages and to teach English to thousands of women and children who come to the wells.

If you would like to share your stories with us, give feedback about the book, contact us for interviews or speaking engagements, or order books from us, you may email us at *gaev5@yahoo.com.*

- Jim and Jerry

Made in the USA
Lexington, KY
19 January 2018